# MY EXPERIENCE WITH A JEZEBEL SPIRIT EXPOSED

SHAWNA HUSKEY

Copyright © 2024 Shawna Lashae Huskey

ALL RIGHTS RESERVED. This book contains material protected under International and Federal Copyright Laws and Treaties. Any unauthorized reprint or use of this material is prohibited. No part of this book may be reproduced or transmitted in any form or by any means, electronic or mechanical, including photocopying, recording, or by any information storage and retrieval system without express written permission from the author/publisher.

Zondervan NIV Study Bible (K. L. Barker, Ed.; Full rev. ed.). (2002). Zondervan.

Scripture is taken from the New King James Version®. Copyright © 1982 by Thomas Nelson. All rights reserved.

Book Cover Design: Prize Publishing House

Printed by Prize Publishing House, LLC in the United States of America.

First printing edition 2024.

Prize Publishing House
P.O. Box 9856, Chesapeake, VA 23321

www.PrizePublishingHouse.com

Library of Congress Control Number: 2024911955

ISBN (Paperback): 979-8-9908345-0-7
ISBN (E-Book): 979-8-9908345-1-4

*"Rev. Shawna Huskey takes readers on a journey with her soul-baring account of a troubling encounter with a Jezebel spirit."*
**- Shawn Whitsell, Writer/Director**

*"Rev. Shawna Huskey wants her readers to know and realize that the Jezebel spirit is real, but they can have victory over it."*
**- Ford Huskey, Pastor of Powerhouse Ministries**

*"Insightful and informative Pastor Shawna Huskey fearlessly shares her experience with the Jezebel spirit. Pastor Shawna Huskey gives Biblical insight and Godly guidance on how to discern and deal with this cunning, controlling, and manipulative spirit without succumbing to its grasp."*
**- Evangelist Tia Roach**

# Contents

Introduction ................................................................. ix

Chapter 1 ..................................................................... 1

Chapter 2 ..................................................................... 5

Chapter 3 ..................................................................... 9

Chapter 4 ................................................................... 13

Chapter 5 ................................................................... 15

Chapter 6 ................................................................... 19

Chapter 7 ................................................................... 25

Chapter 8 ................................................................... 29

Chapter 9 ................................................................... 33

References ................................................................. 37

# Introduction

Growing up in a Pentecostal church, I remember hearing the name Jezebel, but it was associated with red dresses, red lipstick, jewelry and makeup, and a fast-tailed girl, as the old folk used to say. I found out in my adult life that it was much more than what I had heard about. It was an entire demon from hell.

I felt led by God to write this book about my experience with the Jezebel spirit. I pray that I can help someone deal with the same spirit in hopes that they understand that these spirits are real. They operate in our churches and sometimes destroy them because many leaders do not recognize this spirit. Many people do not even believe that this spirit exists. This spirit exists not only in women but also in men. This spirit operates not only in the church but at our jobs, in our governments, and anywhere else this demonic force can try to carry out Satan's agenda on earth.

As God revealed this demonic spirit to me, He told me to write, and that is what I did. Sometimes, there is a demon operating behind a person with a smile. They may seem genuine and harmless and say all the right things. They may seem righteous on the outside, but on the inside, they are evil. This demon comes to disrupt the Kingdom of God and deceive as many as it can.

To detect these spirits, we must ask God to give us discernment and wisdom. To discern is to distinguish between good and evil, truth and falsehood. Wisdom is the ability to discern or judge what is true and right and then put that understanding into practice in your daily life. (*Wisdom*, King James Dictionary Online, 2024). If you do not have either of the two, pray and ask God to give it to you because you will need it in these last and evil days.

# Chapter 1

Jezebel was the daughter of Ethbaal, who was the King of Sidon and Tyre for thirty-two years. He killed his brother and took over the throne. He was the priest of the cult Baal, known as the "lord." Baal is the Canaanite Phoenician god of fertility, rain, and storms. He is also associated with Beelzebub, demons, sacrificing children, and perverted sexual rituals. In the Bible, Baal is described as a false god or idol. They also worshiped the false goddess Asherah.

Jezebel married the King of Israel, Ahab, and influenced him to worship Baal. Ahab built altars of Baal in the temple of Baal in Samaria (1 Kings 16:32) and then made an Asherah pole in verse 33. The Bible did not have anything nice to say about this woman. It sounds like she followed in her father's footsteps promoting Baal.

She was an enemy of God. She was a very cunning, spiritually controlling, conniving, dangerous, vicious, and violent woman. Jezebel did not waste any time after she married Ahab. One of her first acts was killing the Lord's prophets in 1 Kings

18:4. In 1 Kings 21:1-16, Ahab wanted to buy a man named Naboth's vineyard, but he refused to sell. He told Jezebel about it, and she and two others plotted against Naboth and lied on him, falsely accusing him of blaspheming God. He was stoned to death. Ahab took possession of the vineyard.

According to 2 Kings 9:22, she was also into witchcraft and sorcery. *"And it came to pass when Joram saw Jehu, and he said, is it peace? And he answered what peace, so long as the whoredoms of thy mother Jezebel and her witchcraft are so many?"* When I think of witchcraft, it is the practice of casting spells, magic, hexes, and potions for evil purposes.

She influenced the Israelites so much that later, Jesus addresses the church of Thyatira in Revelations 2:20, *"But I have this against you: You tolerate that woman Jezebel, who calls herself a prophetess. By her teaching, she misleads My servants to be sexually immoral and to eat food sacrificed to idols."* She encouraged the people in the church to practice sexual immorality and idolatry. She seduced the servants to commit sex acts with idol worship. She allowed a common practice of eating food that was dedicated to idols.

Jezebel's greatest enemy was Prophet Elijah; he came against her evil rule. He confronted Ahab. He had a showdown at Mount Carmel with 850 prophets who ate at Jezebel's table. He had them all slaughtered; when Jezebel heard this, she sent word to have him killed, but he fled and hid in a cave; meanwhile, God raised up another King, Jehu, and commanded him to take Ahab and his whole family out. In 2 Kings 9, Jehu did just that and wiped Ahab's whole family out, including Ahab's wife, Jezebel.

She died a very gruesome death. When she knew he was coming, she put on her makeup and fixed her hair. I was wondering if she was going to try to seduce Jehu. She asked him if he came in peace. Instead, Jehu asked, "Who is on my side?" The eunuchs looked out, and he had her eunuchs throw her out the window, and the Bible said that her blood splattered everywhere, and the horses trampled over her. Jehu went to eat and drink. When they went back to bury her, there was nothing left but her skull, feet, and hands. The dogs had eaten her body (2 Kings 9:30-37).

# Chapter 2

My husband and I met this lady, Narcissa. Narcissa wanted to have a women's conference at our church because the church she was currently attending did not accept women ministers. So, my husband, the pastor, allowed her to have it at our church. We started seeing her visiting our church more and more. We loved her. She seemed sweet, and she seemed on fire for God. Narcissa was also a minister, so we invited her to the pulpit every time she visited our church.

In 2018, my mom got sick. She had to have a tumor removed from her brain. She started having strokes in her brain after the surgery, which caused her to become brain-dead. With broken hearts, my sisters and I had to decide to take her off the ventilator. My mother passed shortly after. My mother lived in Madisonville, Kentucky, where we had her funeral. Madisonville, Kentucky, is a little over an hour from Bowling Green, where we lived. At the funeral, my church family traveled, and I looked back and saw Narcissa there. I thought, "Wow," because it was so sweet and thoughtful of her to travel all that way for me and my family, and she really did not know us.

As time went on, she eventually joined our church and immediately wanted to work. My husband and I were definitely excited because we got a good worker. My husband put her over a couple of ministries in the church. She seemed to work them well. Everything seemed to be going well with her.

I worked for a factory. Narcissa told me she had put an application in where I worked. I said, "Well, I hope you get the job." Well, she ended up getting the job. I was so happy for her at the time. Still, everything seemed good with her.

When it was my husband's Pastor's Anniversary, she picked me up at my house and drove me to get my hair done. We talked the whole way there, while getting my hair done, and back. It seemed like I had known her forever. I believe I even posted about it on Facebook at the time, not knowing this was the beginning of my troubles.

She did not waste any time. She started asking me who oversaw the Women's Ministry, the kitchen, and this and that. Then she said she was going to join the praise team. It was almost like she wanted to oversee the things she was asking about. It was very strange.

Later, my husband and I were celebrating our wedding anniversary, so we decided to stay in town and get a hotel. If I am not mistaken, my husband had called my friend/armor bearer to decorate the hotel room. My armor bearer called

Narcissa to come to help her decorate our hotel room. When we walked in, there were pictures of us everywhere; there were pictures on the mirrors, on the desk, and on the jacuzzi tub. I thought it was very cute, but my spirit was saying something different. My spirit was very troubled. I did not know why at the time, but I brushed it off. I thought maybe I was feeling that way because I still did not really know her.

Then, one day, one of my husband's friends, who knew and dealt with her, called him about Narcissa. They had lunch together, and he ended up telling him to be careful with her. He told him several things that she would do if she did not get her way and how she wanted to be the First Lady without being married to the Pastor. My husband and I would always give people the benefit of the doubt, but I definitely started watching and was prayerful. I began to see little things with her that would just vex my spirit. Still, at the time, I really did not know why or what was really going on. I started to notice that when my armor bearer and I were talking and laughing, I would look back at her, and she would have a funny look on her face. It was a look of jealousy. It was very weird.

# Chapter 3

Later, I was diagnosed with uterine fibroids, so I ended up having surgery. I was out of work on paid sick leave. I was getting paid, but it was not normal pay. Our household was struggling a little bit, but God took care of us. One day in church, the pastor/my husband was talking about how God was taking care of us in the midst of what was going on. Apparently, Narcissa asked how much our rent was at the time. She wrote us a $1,000 check in the middle of service. *Wow,* I was thinking, *who does that?* That had to be God because who just gives that kind of money freely is what I was thinking.

I did not know then, but the more I studied Jezebel's spirit, the more I realized there may be a motive behind it. I thought of Proverbs 13:22, which says, "The wealth of the wicked is reserved for the righteous." He will use the wealth of the wicked and bless his people.

At Christmas, I decided to have a Christmas party with the women at the church. Everyone was eating and fellowshipping.

When I was about to start the games, Narcissa got up and said she was going home. She said she was tired. I thought that was very strange, and why did she even come?

Another incident occurred when I did a live stream of a Woman's conference. She said she was coming, but then suddenly, she had a headache. I started to think that she never participated in anything I did. All the women exchanged Christmas gifts, but she did not participate. I thought, wow, she does not support anything. But oh well. Still, I am trying to give her the benefit of a doubt.

When the pandemic hit in 2020, we had to close the church. She told me that the pastor needed to do this; he needed to do that. By this time, I was a little aggravated with her. I let her know that I am sure that he knows what he should do. I believed that she wanted to be in charge. I found out she had a whole page of her side ministry. The more I was around her, my spirit became more vexed, but I kept praying. We began doing church services on Facebook Live and parking lot services. One day, we pulled up, and she was walking around the parking lot praying. My spirit was troubled. It literally messed my spirit up. I started praying and asking God what in the world is going on. *Why am I so vexed? Is it me?* I heard Him say, "Watch and pray."

Things began to get weirder and stranger the more I watched and prayed. My husband and I would stand at the end of the road and wave to people as they were leaving the parking lot after services. One day, I saw her standing and waving at everyone like she was Miss America. I kept thinking and seeing weird behavior concerning her. There was a time when one of our decorators was asking me about some decorations, asking me if I liked them and if it was okay to put them in a certain place, and the lady was standing there with us. Well, she answered before I could get it out; she said, "That's fine," and I guess she caught herself. She was like, "Oh, I'm answering for you." Our decorator looked at her like she was crazy. The more I prayed, the more I started seeing more and more.

She started inboxing me, always asking me how the pastor/my hubby was doing to the point where I just asked her if I had missed something. And, of course, I did not get a response. One time, we were in the middle of church service, and I got an inbox from her asking about the pastor/my hubby losing weight. She was commenting on my post, talking about how his beard looks good, just irritating me. It was like she was trying to provoke me into anger. This is one of the characteristics of the Jezebel spirit that I will mention as you read.

I just kept praying. Everything about her really started to trouble my spirit: her Facebook posts, her pictures—she would post a lot of pictures of herself.

# Chapter 4

Our church ended up going back to the sanctuary with limited capacity. People began to come in and join the ministry before and during the pandemic, and that is when the problems really began to arise.

Women were accepting their calling to preach. So, the lady started not liking the new ministers. She really didn't like one of them. I'm not sure why or if she thought they were getting close to me and hubby. They were a married couple, and we clicked with them. I guess she didn't like anyone getting close to us. She came up to me asking me what I thought of one of the new ministers because she had asked what the pastor had said to her about something he had asked her. I told her, "Well, I don't really know her." But as she was talking to me, her eyes were moving fast from side to side; at the time, I thought this was weird, but I remember turning away from her because it was just too creepy. God later revealed to me that she was giving me the evil eye. The evil eye is believed to be a curse that is given by a person who has negative intentions. I'm not sure what her evil intentions were, maybe to turn me against the woman or for me to come up under her spell, but it didn't work. It literally messed me up when God revealed that to me.

As time went on, during a church service, I saw Narcissa lay hands on this one woman, grab her face, and look her in the eyes. (EVIL EYE) It was almost like she was trying to hypnotize her, as weird as it sounds. When that woman got up, she was mesmerized by this woman. She started following her like a puppy. It was very strange and vexed my spirit. The Lord revealed that she had been bewitched. Bewitch means "to be out of one's mind," "to astonish," and "to overwhelm with wonder." (Kapp, 2024). The Greek word baskaino means to" fascinate by false representation.

Also to bring evil on one by feigned praise or an evil eye, to charm, bewitch one." (Strong's Greek Lexicon, 2024). In Galatians 3:1, Paul called the Galatians foolish and asked them who had bewitched them. Basically, asking them who cast their evil eye on them and led them away from their faith in the gospel. It blew my mind that something like this could even happen.

There was a time when the pastor was talking to her, and she was smiling and batting her eyelashes. She had lashes really flapping I'll never forget. My armor bearer saw it, and she asked me, "Did you see that?" I said, "Yes, ma'am, I sure did." It went all over me. I thought, *Oh, she was flirting with my hubby right in front of me,* but I knew it was much more than that and didn't trip off it. I've dealt with those types as long as I've been a pastor's wife, and I wasn't worried one bit.

# Chapter 5

As church started going on and people began to come in, Covid hit our church. My husband/pastor had got it, and we had to sleep in separate rooms for 14 days (about two weeks), and that's when God began to speak to me about this whole situation. I had someone send me a video of the pastor talking about the Leviathan spirit, and I took notes. It opened my eyes to some of these demonic spirits. The Bible talks about Leviathan in Job 41. It is a sea serpent known as the spirit of pride.

According to waragainstevil.org, "some of the characteristics of a Leviathan spirit are:

- It twists the truth.
- It breaks covenants.
- It severs the relationship with God.
- It is stiff-necked.
- It is hard-hearted and cold.
- It blocks communication with the Holy Spirit.

- It is proud, arrogant, and haughty.
- It is a whispering liar.
- It is contentious.
- It lifts leaders to destroy them.
- Depression.
- Blame and self-pity."

One of the characteristics of this spirit that I saw in Narcissa right off the bat was stiff-necked. A stiff-necked person is stubborn and believes they know more than anyone. They won't participate in anything unless it's their idea first. I was reminded when I had the live stream women's conference and the Christmas party, and when our women exchanged gifts, she didn't participate. I also noticed the proud, haughty, and arrogant characteristics of Narcissa. The Leviathan spirit operates through a spirit of pride, which leads to a sense of false identity and power. This causes a person to worship themselves, which is idolatry. One thing I saw in Narcissa was that she was very arrogant; if you looked at her social media, there would be many pictures of her; it was weird. I also noticed the blame and self-pity characteristic in her concerning certain situations and telling half-truths.

God had me studying more of these different types of spirits. God had me study the Python spirit as well. This one blew my mind. The Python spirit squeezes the life out of the believer. The Python spirit is the spirit behind divination. Divination means foretelling future events. The Greek word for divination is "Putin," which means python. I'm reminded of the story of the slave girl in the Bible in Acts 16. She had the spirit of divination, and she followed and taunted Paul and Silas, trying to distract them from their assignment. She was speaking accurately but out of the wrong spirit, and Paul was annoyed and cast the spirit out of her.

The major traits of the python spirit are:

- "It squeezes the life out of their victims.
- It loves flattery.
- It demands attention.
- It loves to be seen and heard.
- It wants to be important.
- There is a monetary motive.
- It blends in and behaves like the people around." (Hyatt, 2018)

This messed me up. I also saw several Python spirit traits in Narcissa. She always loved to be seen, and she would be up during the whole service, walking and recording. She also operated in divination. She would give people words and it would be accurate, but the spirit operating was false. I'm like, *God, what is really going on?*

I was still in quarantine, and I came across a video from a well-known prophet for the nation. He was talking about witchcraft. He said that every time he would be around witches, he would get a headache. He said you would feel it in your body. I was like, *wow, God.* When I got around Narcissa, I would get sick to my stomach. I would be very uneasy in my spirit. It seemed like I was seeing and going through everything he was talking about. I just cried and cried. I had never dealt with something like this. He was talking about the spirit of Jezebel, and that's when I knew I had to study this one, too. Come to find out the Leviathan, the Python, and the Jezebel spirits work together in the kingdoms of darkness to destroy lives and nations.

# Chapter 6

The Jezebel spirit is a wicked, cunning, seducing, provoking, manipulative spirit that is often associated with females but can manifest in anyone, just like the woman in the Bible. From studying these spirits, it is a spirit that tries to destroy churches, families, people, and God's prophets, especially God's prophet.

"Some characteristics of the Jezebel spirit are:

- It seeks to gain popularity and favor with people of influential and high positions of leadership.
- It will seek out other individuals they feel are 'weaker' to become followers of them.
- It is never humble. Whenever this spirit receives praise, it always responds in false humility.
- It is defensive and combative whenever confronted about anything.
- It loves to teach and seeks to gain control in every situation.

- It wants to be seen as the most spiritual and powerful one.
- It typically loves to pray elaborate, long prayers.
- It will not submit to authority.
- It loves to pray and impart evil demonic spirits into others, especially in the church.
- It hates the voice of the prophet and seeks to control and destroy those who operate in the prophetic.
- It plays the victim.
- It provokes then blames you.
- It will never repent." (LLqwyd, 2014)

I saw these traits in Narcissa as well, just about all of them. Like I said earlier, she had blessed us with $1,000. I believed that there was a motive behind it to gain favor and popularity with us. In the beginning, she seemed as if she was genuine. The provoking, as I mentioned earlier, I would pick it up in the spirit. Another characteristic I saw was that she immediately started seeking people to follow her, and she was able to get a few. Everywhere she went, someone followed her.

She always acted like she was the most spiritual and powerful one. I remember one time, some other ministers and I were praying, and we left; she had to stay and give the lady a word. Narcissa also loved to preach and teach. She would make live videos every day teaching. She would say to us that if we needed anyone to preach and teach, she was always available. After studying this spirit, I would say that was a red flag for sure.

Narcissa pretty much did her own thing to fit her own agenda. The Jezebel spirit loves to pray and impart evil demonic spirits. Narcissa was always praying for people and imparting evil spirits. It would disturb my spirit so badly. I would often pray and cover the people she was preying on. Yes, preying on! Narcissa would play victim concerning issues with a past relationship she claimed to be in. She always blamed the other parties and never owned up to the part she played in the situation.

This spirit co-labors with rebellion, witchcraft, pride, offense, manipulation, seduction, idolatry, dominance, religion, fear, intimidation, insecurity, jealousy, bitterness, unfairness, deception, and competition. (DeGraw, 2019). Its seducing spirit persuades people away from God by connecting with hurts, pains, spiritual needs, and itching ears, wanting to hear a word from God and not wanting to wait for God's voice.

The Jezebel spirit operates with a divination spirit. As I said earlier. This means that they may prophesy something correctly, but it's not coming from the spirit of God. It's coming from a demonic spirit. The Jezebel spirit loves to form little groups of people to build her influence in the person she is trying to teach. Many times, the pastor of the church she is in doesn't authorize these meetings. I learned that Narcissa would have meetings teaching the other ladies.

I felt led to share what I had learned about these spirits on Facebook; I was getting so many inboxes that I got phone calls about these different spirits. I did a whole study on the

Jezebel spirit on Facebook. I saw others talking about this spirit. I would get on a few Facebook Lives, and they would talk about this spirit. I thought, *the Jezebel spirit is manifesting itself all over the world.*

When I started posting about it, I got so much feedback that I did part one and part two. People had experienced the spirit or were going through with the spirit at the time. I was exhausted because I felt like I was in the fight of my life. When you begin to come into the knowledge of the spirits, they begin to attack you. That's what was happening to me. I entered spiritual warfare.

The more I studied and fasted, God began to reveal more and more about the spirit influencing Narcissa. *It's all starting to make sense to me now. That is exactly what I was seeing.* I saw all these characteristics in her. She had formed her little groups and started causing confusion behind the scenes in the church. She had certain people against certain ministers. I would see her taking women out to another room at church, praying for them, and ministering to them.

As God revealed this to me, I was messed up every Sunday. I felt like I was going crazy because I felt like no one was understanding what I was seeing and going through. I just kept praying. The more God revealed, the more I started to think about all the things that had happened so far. She would take pictures with me, and of course, at those times, I didn't really think anything of it. I was looking through my photos, and I saw all kinds of pictures of us. She wanted to be close to me and take me out at the same time. I just could not believe it. She didn't like any of the ministerial staff, except the ones she thought agreed with her lies.

We had a minister and a young boy join at the same time. Well, the spirit was very high that day, and everyone was rejoicing. God told me to look at her. I remember her being in the very back, crossing her arms like she was mad; she never stood up or seemed to be happy. I did not understand that.

When confronted about a job she was not doing at the church, she was very defensive. She blamed everyone else but herself. There came a time when every time I was around her, or if she spoke, I would get sick to my stomach. I would often see darkness on her. I also would see a black cloud over her. Her skin color began to look dark to me. She preached one Sunday, and all I could see was black on her face. I was sick to my stomach the whole time. I was watching the congregation, and it seemed all the people were cheering and clapping except me. I was sitting down, praying that God would open the people's eyes. He did some.

# Chapter 7

I continued to fast and pray. I was literally in church and at home, lying on my face, crying some days. I kept praying that God would continue to reveal. I felt like I was in a spiritual battle. It was like the enemy knew it was being exposed. I continued to pray and fast.

We had an initial sermon service for one of our members, and she came, and my wait was over for more revelations from God. The final straw for me - I was up in front singing with the praise team, and Narcissa was sitting almost in front of me. I looked at her, and I saw a demon manifest. The face was burnt, and it was not her eyes; they were red. I watched, and I saw the demon was looking at my husband. He had got up doing something, and that demon turned and looked at him almost like a robot. It literally messed me up because I had never seen one manifest before. I had heard about them and believed they did exist, but I had never seen one. All I could say was Jesus. When I said Jesus, her face changed back to normal. I didn't even tell anyone what I saw at first, not even my husband. I was messed up the rest of the night. I just prayed; that was all I could do.

The next day, I was praying and asking God what in the world was going on. He revealed to me that she was sent to terminate me. I immediately broke down crying right at work. I was like, "God, why? I have been nothing but nice to her." God said, "The terminator, who is the enemy, is assigned to terminate your character, terminate your assignments from God, and terminate your dreams." I ended up posting this on Facebook. I ended up calling my husband at work, and I just cried again, and I told him what I saw at church and what God told me. That night, I got more confirmation through my hubby. We were having prayer calls just about every night. And he began to talk about the movie *The Terminator*. So, the Terminator in the movie is sent to kill this woman who, in the future, was going to give birth to a son who was going to change the world. In every *Terminator* movie, the Terminator gets stronger and harder to kill. As he was talking, I was balling because he just opened it up more to me. After all, the enemy will send terminators to assassinate you, and each demon gets stronger.

See, the Jezebel spirit is one of Satan's higher-ranking, intelligent demons. If you do not have a high spirit of discernment, you will not recognize this spirit. As this spirit was still at our church, I continued to pray, fast, and cover the church body. At the end of 2020, we had a night watch service. I fasted and prayed again for revelation during the week of service.

## My Experience with a Jezebel Spirit

December 31, 2020, revealed even more of this woman. I thought she was acting strange. She sat in the back. I had her down to do the scripture, even though I was uneasy about putting her up to do anything. She did her scripture, and I watched her walk to the back and grab her purse and keys like she was leaving. She stood back by the door like she was scared. As I was looking at her, her whole face changed; the demon had manifested again, and this time, it looked like the shape of an alien face. Sounds crazy, but I saw this in the spirit. Anytime the spirit is high, you will see a demon manifest right before your eyes. I could not believe what I was seeing.

Not only did I see Narcissa at church but also at my job. As I stated earlier, I would see her just about every day at work, and I began to avoid her. I did not want any parts of this spirit. At times, she would work close to my department, and I would often see her in the bathroom; I ended up dodging her even then. She would message me and say, "I see you." I would say to her, "Where are you?" because I never saw her, nor was I looking for her. When she did not work close, sometimes she would manage to get up to my department bathroom. I would ask, "Are you working close?" She would say, "No, in the back." I am thinking, *Are there no bathrooms back there*? There was a time when we worked over, and I guess her department did not. I was working. I looked back; she was right behind me; she did not even let me know she was there. Quite creepy, huh?

Then, it seemed as if she was stalking me. I kept thinking, *Am I being stalked, or am I going crazy?* I had a co-worker call her my stalker, so I am like, maybe there is something to this. She knew where I parked, and she would wait in the parking lot in the mornings until I got there. It was almost like she knew my every move. In my studies, I found out this spirit will stalk those they envy and try to get every little detail about a person they hate and use the information against them. She started buying me gifts; she brought donuts and a T-shirt for me at work, and I threw them away. Anything that was given to us by her, I threw it all away.

I appreciated the gifts, but after seeing the demon working and manifesting in her, I did not want anything from her. This is another trait of the Jezebel spirit. They often give gifts like money, clothes, and anything to gain favor with those who have influence so they can be allowed to operate in the ministry. It is manipulation. Also, some gifts carry curses; we must be very careful when accepting gifts from everyone. We must pray and discern.

# Chapter 8

God revealed what I was dealing with, so I started praying on what to do. She began to miss service sometimes, and every time she was not there, the spirit was so high.

Later, on a Saturday, I heard that she was walking around the sanctuary like she was praying. It went all over me. I started praying, and God told me to get to church early the next day. God told me to anoint every chair in the sanctuary, the doors that everyone comes in, the nursery room, and to pray. I was anointing everything and crying. Then, God told me to pray during the service Sunday. I began to pray, and the Holy Ghost took over. I went into a spiritual warfare prayer. God had me calling different spirits out. Then I started commanding them to go and commanding the Jezebel spirits to go. The spirit got so high that I was in awe of what God was doing. Then I saw the spirit operating in Narcissa start acting. She was bouncing around; one time, I saw her walk to the back and then back up to the front. She opened the door to the sanctuary. The spirit was so high; several things were happening all at once. I looked up at her again and saw she had her back against the wall. Her eyes were moving fast, almost like she was scared. That demonic spirit had manifested, and people were starting to see it but really were not aware of what it was. One person was asking us what was wrong with her.

The next weekend, Saturday, she was at the feeding ministry. They met every other Saturday to feed the community. I was there because I had praise team practice. Well, I heard a bunch of prayer going on downstairs; someone had come and told me Narcissa was down there and laying hands. It went all over me. By this time, I am covering the women and the church. I went down there just to see what was going on. When I got down there, I saw Narcissa with her hands on another woman praying and another lady praying. The woman that they were praying for was having back issues at the time. My spirit was so vexed. I immediately began to pray in tongues. I went into a warfare prayer again. I am not sure what I was speaking, but her hands came off the woman; the Jezebel spirit backed all the way up. It messed me up; I found out at that moment that I really had power and authority in the spirit. The Bible lets us know we have authority over demons. I told the women down there that I was covering them in prayer. I said something along the lines of demons laying hands on people. It just came out, but it was true. I was so upset and fed up with this spirit at that time. I went upstairs to the sanctuary and cried out to the Lord like I had never cried out before. At the time, I called some other ladies, and they were praying with me. My heart was torn up because I felt like she was deceiving many. I mean, she almost had me fooled, but I knew something was up the more I was around her and talked to her.

After the kitchen episode, she came back one more Sunday, all over the place in people's ears. Like I said earlier, they love to pray and impart their demonic spirits to others. This is why you must be careful who lays hands on you or imparts in you. Spirits are transferable if you are not careful. I prayed to God and said, "Please, I cannot take it anymore." Well, she ended up having a meeting with the pastor. I told him I could not go to the meeting; I would have blasted her, so I thought it was best I did not go in. And I was still trying to wrap my head around all of this. She ended up telling the pastor she was leaving or taking a break. She ended up taking a couple of people with her, who fell into her trap. Not only did she leave the ministry, but she quit the job, too.

This is what happens when you fight in the spirit. The Lord heard my prayers and moved her out of my way and life. The last time I saw her on the job, she walked right past my area. I had not even seen her enter my area in a while, and she walked by, looking at me very evilly. I acted like I did not see her because I was pretty much avoiding her by then. However, I began to pray that God remove her because she had vexed my spirit so badly that morning. I never saw her again at work. I eventually heard that she had quit, and I was like, *wow, God, you moved quickly after I prayed that prayer*. I was thanking God and trying to hold back tears all day at work. When I got in my car after work, I sat there and just cried my eyes out. God had finally moved. I will never forget that moment. I felt so free and felt like I had got the victory over the enemy.

# Chapter 9

God told me to write a book about this. He said it will heal you as you write. Right then, I knew I had not let it go or that I was not healed from this. I was so hurt that someone could be evil like this and want to take my place and eliminate me. I was nothing but nice.

I saw her once again, and I did not know how I was going to react because I was still feeling betrayed, hurt, and mad. I walked right by her and did not speak. God was whooping me for not speaking and made me apologize. I did it out of obedience to my father, but when I did, I felt a whole weight lifted. I was really freed from this; I ended up blocking her from social media and my phone.

This is my experience with the Jezebel spirit. It lasted over two years, and then God intervened. This is when God showed me who I was in the kingdom—a prophet and a spokesman for God. I was being attacked because I could see the demon. I was a threat to the kingdom of darkness.

The Jezebel spirit is still lurking in churches today. Most often, you will find it in leadership. The Jezebel spirit still hates true prophets of God because they can see through her and confront her lies. The true prophets can see the demon behind the person that no one else sees. God gives them insight. This is why the church needs prophets today. Please do not shut their voices down. Silencing the prophets will cause this spirit to be hidden and not be noticed until it is too late and destruction hits.

If you are dealing with this spirit, make sure you fast and stay prayed up. God will give you wisdom on how to deal with this spirit. It is not an easy task. We are in a spiritual battle. We are not fighting flesh. We must fight in the spirit. The Bible tells us in Ephesians 6:12-13, *"For we wrestle not against flesh and blood, but against principalities, against powers, against the rulers of the darkness of the world, against spiritual wickedness in high places."*

You may even see these characteristics within yourself. I do believe no one is so beyond reach for God to save. Even though Jezebel in the Bible would not repent, I believe that anyone can be delivered. The first thing you must do is repent. It means to change one's mind and purpose: regret. Renouncing any legal rights - legal rights of giving demons an opportunity to enter or harass you, allowing the demons that have been invited in (sins, unforgiveness, soul ties, trauma, idolatry, curses). (*Repent*, King James Dictionary Online, 2024).

Command the demons to leave. You can tell the demons that they have no legal right to stay attached to you, and they must leave in the name of Jesus Christ. (Great Bible Study, 2024).

# References

"12 Characteristics of a Leviathan Spirit: How to Recognize and Overcome It." https://waragainstevil.org/12-characteristics-of-a-leviathan-spirit/. Retrieved 17 June 2024.

DeGraw, Kathy. "Why It's So Hard to Cast Out a Jezebel Spirit." Charisma. 20 May 2019. https://mycharisma.com/spiritled-living/spiritual-warfare/why-it-s-so-hard-to-cast-out-a-jezebel-spirit/. Retrieved 23 May 2024.

"Demonic Legal Rights." Great Bible Study. 2024. https://www.greatbiblestudy.com/deliverance-ministry/demonic-legal-rights/. Retrieved 17 June 2024.

G940 - baskainō - Strong's Greek Lexicon (KJV). https://www.blueletterbible.org/lexicon/g940/kjv/tr/0-1/. Retrieved 17 June 2024.

Hyatt, Eddie. "5 Major Traits of the Python Spirit." End Time Headlines. 2018. https://endtimeheadlines.org/2018/09/5-major-traits-of-the-python-spirit/. Retrieved 17 June 2024.

Kapp, Jacob W. *Bewitch*. International Standard Bible Encyclopedia Online. 2024. https://www.internationalstandardbible.com/B/bewitch.html. Retrieved 17 June 2024.

King James Dictionary. *Repent*. Bible Study Tools. 2024. All rights reserved. https://www.biblestudytools.com/dictionaries/king-james-dictionary/repent. Retrieved 17 June 2024.

King James Dictionary. *Wisdom*. Bible Study Tools. 2024. All rights reserved. https://www.biblestudytools.com/dictionaries/king-james-dictionary/wisdom. Retrieved 17 June 2024.

Llqwyd. McHugh & Chen Mediation Specialists. "Exposing the Spirit of Jezebel." 14 November 2014. https://conflictmediate.com/exposing-the-spirit-of-jezebel-10-characteristics-of-the-jezebel-spirit/. Retrieved 19 June 2024.

www.ingramcontent.com/pod-product-compliance
Lightning Source LLC
Chambersburg PA
CBHW060628030426
42337CB00018B/3250